A SONG, HALF & HALF
(Love Poems)

A SONG, HALF & HALF

(Love Poems)

From the Amazon Bestselling Author
Nandini Sahu

Black Eagle Books
2022

Black Eagle Books
USA address:
7464 Wisdom Lane
Dublin, OH 43016

India address:
E/312, Trident Galaxy, Kalinga Nagar,
Bhubaneswar-751003, Odisha, India

E-mail: info@blackeaglebooks.org
Website: www.blackeaglebooks.org

First International Edition Published by
Black Eagle Books, 2022

A SONG, HALF & HALF (Love Poems)
by **Nandini Sahu**

Copyright © Nandini Sahu

All rights reserved. No part of this publication may be reproduced, stored in a retrieval system, or transmitted, in any form or by any means, electronic, mechanical, photocopying, recording or otherwise without the prior permission of the publisher.

Cover Photo: **Nandini Sahu**
Interior Design: Ezy's Publication

ISBN- 978-1-64560-256-9 (Paperback)
Library of Congress Control Number: 2022933811

Printed in the United States of America

from
Ocean
to
Ocean

Preface

"Paradise is attained by touch."
-- Helen Keller in *Divining the Body*

Words have their own culture. They are independent once they are written, they have their own path. But before creating those words, the writers form their own course under the guidance of some divine agenda called love. Of late, I have been thinking a lot about love and God as counterparts working towards eternity-- a love that is unrequited, a love that has no boundaries. The saplings come out gloriously only when the earth cracks open;thus, life culminates only when love happens. Love is the touchstone to deify life. Now I sense, I am the apex of love, and this is my state of being. I would rather go with this quest for love till my last breath.

A Song, Half and Half is a selection of my love poems written between 14th February 2021 to 14th February 2022. Life has never been as eventful as these few months— some mystical waiting of years came to an end during this period. And then I had the most hectic yet fulfilling academic accomplishments in March 2021—with multiple academic lectures and launch of a new academic programme, *MA in Folklore and Culture Studies*, designed by me singlehandedly, creating ripples in academics. Then in mid-2021 I shifted to my 'home', to the home of my own; moving from government accommodations and rented houses, now I have a home, a room and a table of my own. And then in mid-2021, I succumbed to Covid. I was confined to my bed, isolated; I faced low oxygen levels to worst nightmares, near-death situations and mood swings. And then, poetry became my therapy, one poem a day became my survival strategy. Now after my complete recovery, I look back at the previous year with awe. And then there was this moment of epiphany in early 2022, submerging my being in the Pacific, when I decided to publish my love poems as a collection, A Song, Half and Half. When I gave this proposal to my erudite publisher Mr. Satya Pattanaik, he was happy, and accepted it most proximately. Some of the poems from this collection were originally published in *Selected Poems of Nandini Sahu*, some in some independent journals, and some poems are new—but the tone and tenure of these poems can be condensed to one word—*love*.

All the poems are about my moods, modes and mores, they are about the roller coaster rides that I had, and of course about the most complex human emotions. My readers and researchers may find these poems very different from my earlier poems. Mythical poet, folklorist Nandini writing romantic, jovial, humorous, light poems, while talking about the existential issues at the same time! I have always advocated social mobility literature, Witness Literature, backed with myth and folklore as my poetic tools. The mood of these poems is unlike my other collections. For example, the poem "A Man Like You" professes love for my 'man', my poetic personae, when I am in the best of my moods. The logic behind falling in love with the man is, had I been feeling lonely, low or blue, I would have rather gone to seek therapeutic help. Because a depressed mind will only transfer depression to her/his lover. I preferred to fall in love with 'a man like you' because I am feeling the best of my feelings now—romantic, optimistic, positive—and I pass on these feelings to 'you'. Almost all the poems advocate one such thought, a flickering, flaming emotion, and then the words flow freely. I never edited any of these poems, because somehow, I don't know in what delirious modes I penned these poems. I wrote these poems in a trance, never to look back, edit, re-read, re-write. I kind of renounce my poems once they are written, I detach myself from them and offer them to my august readers to read and give them evenhandedness. There is one poem in this collection, "Ahalya's Waiting". The poem talks about Ahalya vis-à-vis her womanhood. To the myth makers; she was basically a woman cursed by her husband to remain a stone for ages, to be redeemed by Lord Ram. This poem ventures to an alternative reading of Ahalya's character. It backers the need for indulgence of a woman when Ahalya's creator asks her to discover her 'self' all by herself. 'Touch' is used metaphorically in the poem. Ahalya requests her archetypal Lord Ram, if he wants to touch and redeem of her of a 'sin' that she never committed, she would prefer to remain a stone; that would be her ultimate liberation. At the same time she wants her Lord to 'touch' her, if at all, as an elemental man would touch an elemental woman and both of them will complete each other. To me, this is the alternative modernity of myth.

Somewhere I have experimented with humour in some poems — in fact 'humour' has been the most neglected genre in Indian English Poetry. The poem "To Laugh Like You" uses the pun of 'General-Body-Meeting', indicating the meeting of the lovers. And the poem, "A Parody of Love" is a burlesque, it's a travesty of love. In it, the lady is mocking at a pseudo-lover with his toxic masculinity while talking to her true-love, while speaking about the former as a man who wears his gender as an emblem of honour and uses it to try and subvert the woman. A smart, independent, freethinking woman who ignores fools, is too much of a disappointment to the pseudo lover. The poem exposes such people, of course humorously.

Love and the memory of love kept me jovial even during the worst of my covid days. Fever 102, body aches, throat infections, loss of smell and taste and partial hearing, I could bear everything with a smile, teary eyed, but for love. In the first part of the epic poem *Mahabharata*, it is written that the Sage Vyasa asked Lord Ganesha to transcribe the poem as he dictated it to him. Vyasa goes on dictating the *Mahabharatha* with his ideas while Lord Ganesha finished writing the *Mahabharata* in a few days. While I wrote those poems in just a few months, I had almost similar kind of an experience. There was some divine agenda working in my favour, and I heard a voice dictating me these poems. I simply penned those down.

Poetry, as a trade, is honest or otherwise, is not my question here. The variance is that in poetry we tend to conceal much in our passions and gibe those out to reveal poetically. As poets, we are clear about what we are trying to transport to other mediums. *What is History* by E. H. Carr is a book which speaks of the debate over subjectivity and objectivity in times gone by. In fact, no unqualified actuality is history, not even in the myths of medieval or ancient times as they are based upon the discernments of who they were. We can attempt to reach a near historical objectivity and precision depending upon the foundations accessible to us as poets. Once we start writing, if we already have a proposition in mind, like historians, then that piece of writing will be blocked from our vision, with a biased view about race, ethnicity, upbringing, gender, faith, edification, class, etc. In this status quo, we can unquestionably write confessional poetry which could be very near reality based on our individual lives or on life in its universal theme or on the lives of our near and dear ones. It is the subject of a poet -- how much is too much, and what to reveal, and what not to. Thus, this poetry collection, to me, seems so very different from my previous poetry books. Here, I reveal as I conceal. Penned as soliloquies, sometimes in memory of a short-lived love, sometimes re-discovering love in the azure waters of the ocean, and sometimes longing for love, these are my politically incorrect poems. Here I celebrate an unnamed love that is knocking my door, and I am more than willing to leave the door ajar, waiting to renunciate and merge with my love, surrendering like Mirabai surrendered to Lord Krishna.

Many people gave me virtual as well as lived company during my worst times; today I feel fortunate to be alive. I count my blessings. Covid makes you lonelier than ever. When I was craving for human company and my son Sonu (Parthasarathi Sahu) was locked in the other room, we couldn't meet for 14 days. The poor child helplessly called me multiple times from the next room, and I pretended to be fine. I didn't have to be hospitalized, but for his support. My writer friends Dr Anand Prakash, Prof. Santosh Bakaya, Dr.Anita Nahal, Lopa Banerjee, Kalpna Singh Chitnis,Prof. Srilata, Prof. Gopa, Mr. Dinesh Kumar Mali, Prof. Simi, Prof. Asim Siddiqui,Prof.Gopa Ranjan Mishra, Prof.Himanshu Mahapatra, Prof.Amulya Purohit, Prof.SN Tripathy, Sarita Jenamani, Manu Dash, Dr. Roopali Sirkar Gaur, Usha Kishore, Mona Dash, Dr. Shaleen Singh, Dr. Rizio, Dr.Gopi Krishanan Kotoor, Dr. Anamika, Prof.Lakshmishree, Prof.Balaganapathy, Amarendra Khatua Sir, Pina Picolo,

Candice Louisa, Dr. Sunil Sharma, Megha Sood, Dr. Sutanuka, my friends and colleagues Dr. Siddhant Mishra, Dr. Murali, Prof. Vijayshree, Prof S C Garg, Dr. Rakhi, Prof. Ranu Uniyal, Prof. Sanjukta Dasgupta, Dr. Devmalya, Dr. Shivaji, Pooja Priyambada, Prof. Alka, Prof. Smita, Prof. Swati, Prof. Satyanath, Dr. Pema, Dr. Mridula (for so much love and for cooking all that comfort food for me, despite your busy schedule!), Prof. Neera, Prof. Parmod, Prof. Anju, Prof. Malati, Dr. Malathy, Dr. Shikha, Prof. Jitendra, Papuni, Tapan, Rekha, Aruna, Bindu, Papa, Anita, Rita, Najeeb ji, Dr. Anupriya, Dr. Sanjay, Prof. Raj Kumar, Prof. Anil Aneja, Himanshu, Soumya, Sandeep, Sunita -- I thank you for your concern, love and guidance during the worst times. My mother and sisters called me frantically, and I was cranky; they did bear with my mood swings. Mammali, I am your elder sister, but God knows why on earth you and Siwani treat me as your younger sibling, forever, and pamper me! You indulge, spoil me way too much, and let me confess, I enjoy it. Coming to 2022, well, life has more in store for me as far as 'love' is concerned! The other day I told 'him', "You know, I was born to love." He had a beaming smile. Today, I count my blessings. Thank you Arindam-ji, Satya Pattanaik Sir, Dr. Prashant, Dr. Anamika for being there with me. I am the most fortunate teacher to have research scholars like Sagar, Sneha, Pushpa, Devendar, Bhaskar and others for whom I am the teacher, anchor and best friend.

There are some people who read my poems every day, without fail, and sent me honest feedback. Dr. Anand Prakash, whom I simply love, only love, and love a little more every single day, sent me the following feedback. I quote his comments in no specific order on any particular poem:

"I call these poems a statement of assertion in a difficult time. The faith in creativity is paramount. Kudos!... There is a slight change of mood in some poems. A light shadow further brightening the scene. Depth comes with it, a turn to understanding and strength.... Your poetic temperament is transparent! ...The genuine poet cannot hide anything from herself/himself. That is a bright spot of your poetic expression.... The poem 'debt' continues the theme of love from the previous ones. Thus, the word debt has the required positive connotation of loyalty with the lover. I see further improvement on use of words in this poem; they work free from their literality and gain in metaphorical connotation. 'Debt' for that reason is more creative... In this poem, I like the phrases that roll out of imagination with such a rush. Their use is creative, making them fresh with meaning. What is "unabridged heart"? I thought and thought... So much poetic wealth spent in praise of silence. Silence is so fertile and expressive. That is the strength of 'Day after Day'. Hope you would agree... I take this poem as the truthful assertion that you have recovered fully from fever and breath-related issues. Welcome back to the world of health and well-being!... In these poems, I am able to see emerging a new dimension of awareness and self-questioning. That might give added depth to the pursued theme... I am seeing a certain evolution. It began with the emotion, so to say, and moved then on to the realm of thought. At present, it is in the realm of defining things -- selfhood, reciprocity, questioning. I particularly like the progression. What say?... In these two poems, the self questioning and exploration of the love theme continue. Philosophical thought has gradually replaced intense emotion. The question is if it is the way forward or an attempt at the re-evaluation of the experience one went through. I appreciate the thoughtfulness inherent in the poetic pursuit. Wonder if making sense... Am impressed both by your honesty and courage in poetry as well as statement."

Dr. Anand Prakash, if there is a reader like you, which poet will not write poetry, overwhelmed?

During April and May last year, I cried helplessly, vulnerably for days when we lost Padmashree Professor Manoj Das; and then within no time I lost my dearest colleague, Mr.Dhiraj K Sharma, to Covid. He was my co-voyager past two years, he was like family. I spent eight hours a day with him at my workplace. I was shattered to get the news of his sudden death. Sharma ji, I owe a lot to you, you left me too early—I had so many plans with/for you; you will live in the deepest corner and the saddest vacuum of my heart, forever. We failed you. I wish I wasn't a covid patient myself then, to run to you, and give you my service, support, care.

And then, of course, immense gratitude to my *poetic personae*, to the 'Ocean' – I owe you these poems; thank you for being my Muse. I remember my teacher Late Professor Niranjan Mohanty telling me some day, "Love is a human phenomenon—we divinize it by living it." Love, your soothing words have been like life giving oxygen for me; you made this human relationship divine by living some precious moments of life with me. I don't know what future has in store for 'us', but then, I am indebted to you for fleetingly familiarizing me to those finest feelings that incite me to write these poems. I attained *'paradise'* with your Midas *'touch'*, to quote Helen Keller.

Nandini Sahu
14th February 2022

Content

A Man Like You	17
A Parody of Love	19
A Relationship with the Self	21
A Song Written Half and Half	23
A Welcome World	24
Ahalya's Waiting	26
'Alive' and 'Living'	29
Am All Ears to You, Love!	31
An Autumnal Duet	33
And I Am in Love	34
Bottomless	35
Chamomile	37
Day after Day	38
Debt	40
Dreams, these days	42
Epilogue	44
Everything Looks Small from a Certain Height	46
Eyes Well Up	47
Eyes	49
Filling the Molecules	51
Fluency in Silence	53
From Ocean to Ocean	54
Haiku Poems of Love	57
Half of Her Lovers are Half the World Away	58
Has Tomorrow Enough Time?	60
Historical Baggage	62
Hymn to Chant	63
Introspection	65
Is Something Left?	66

Island	68
Isn't Love Enough?	70
Looking Elsewhere this Spring	72
Metaphors	74
Museum	76
My Moods, Modes and Mores	78
My Tranquil City, Tonight	80
No Next Birth	83
Promise of Profusion	84
Reaching the Island	86
Reverie	88
Shipwrecked Souls	89
Small Things Big Things	90
Some But's are So Telling!	91
Spring is the Season	92
Stitching a Love	94
The Fleet-Footed Polar Deer	95
The Lotus Leaf	96
The Maps to Reach You	97
The Sea of Pedigrees	99
The Woman that was Me is Gone	101
Time the Quiet Witness	103
To Laugh Like You	104
Touching You	106
Truth and Gospel Truth	108
We have Earned Our Tomorrow	110
When I Wiped Your Tears	112
World Within A Tree	114
You are Another Me	116
You Before Me	118
You can Never Unknow Me	120
You Own a Piece of Me	121
Your Familiar City	123
Your Fragrance	124

A Man Like You

Did I paint the image of a man like you and secured you to that
canvas, I don't really know. But I know, I tailored myself in.

You may ask me, why did I come to your life in the first place?
"Well, not because I was lonely, depressed,
                        blue or was feeling awfully alone.

For those ailments, there is therapeutic support, isn't it?
                      I sensed my ideal
quest for a man like you when I was feeling the best of my feelings-

contented, romantic, ebullient, jovial, strong, real, feminine.
I wanted to share a segment of those with you,
                      a man like you, in crux."

You treasured that. You cherished when I said, "if someone
comes to our lives with depression, they will only share that. And

if one comes with optimism, that becomes infectious."
Then you resolved that I am the most optimistic woman
                      you have come across.

I love the way you touch me without touching me sometimes
and of course your gentle kisses and ardent touch
                      when you are intense.

I know you will never give up on me even if I am grim or otherwise;
I love your catching giggles and the beam.
                      A man like you is my happy place!

You are unceasingly on my cognizance—if they call it love.
You are the man who can finish not just my sentences,

but my thoughts. Are you my *Stream of Consciousness,*
or that *Objective Correlative* that I live in reverence?

They say the glass is half-empty or half-full,
                                    it's a construal so false!
How about our new narrative my love -- of filling
                                    the quasi-filled glass?

After I had given all my reasons you just winked.
                              As if you knew that you knew
that you knew -- a woman like me is your life time quest,
                                your solitary wish.

A Parody of Love

A parody of love with my love today, about a lampoon.
A caricature of pseudo-love to laugh with my true-love,
                         a burlesque.
That's the fun mood today about this conformist,
ahh his whatsapp status --*'the guardian of ancient civilization'!*

What pompous was he when he met me online
over a lecture I delivered on Culture Studies.
He pretended and pretended to be a part of whatever
I said and did; he called himself even my personal,
                         singular guardian!

He decided that I fell in love with him, as he was so irresistible!
He thought he was attractive and most welcome
                         on my vestibule.
Words of flattery galore, and sycophancy was his syllable.
He simply ordered me to be agreeable, admirable and amicable.

I said, "I don't know you, who the hell are you?" and
he declared that I was only a shy woman,
                         I was not at all disagreeable.
After all, the ornament of a modest woman is being amiable.
He called me, sent mails; he pretended that
my silence was affable.

Love, you are so funny, you created an innovative
                         narrative out of it,
'Love in the Time of Covid' when he offered me gift packets of
Remdesivir, steroids, plasma, Tocilizumab and Favipiravir.
He hated my disinterestedness in his gifts and bouquets of flower.

He declared via emails that he looked great with biceps
which I cannot but admire -- in fact any woman
                              would fall for him.
I didn't pay any heed, he was furious, and demanded--
I would look conspicuous only if we walk together, composed.

How could he have liked that a woman, a mere woman,
didn't value his love, his generosity and his acceptance?
He belongs a to 'School of Thought' where women are
Goddess, Mother-Deities, but not normal respectable creatures.

He believed in the shameless privileges and
                            primacies of the rich.
I could do nothing to erase the feudal mindset.
He stood for hours in front of my house, he was sure
one day I would respond and submit to him, without a doubt.

He used click-baits in his emails, and thumbnail links,
specially designed to catch my attention and to entice me.
He tempted me with promises of awards,
                            as if I looked for those!
Deceptive, sensationalized, misleading stuff he sent in profusely.

Love you don't belong to this world,
                            it's a foul world of hegemony.
You believe in reverence for a woman here and now, not just
in the *femme* idol in a temple.
                            You wish to punish this man of false agony.
I assure you, fools are better ignored,
                            for them you can't create an ebony.

A Relationship with the Self

When life comes apart in your hands
when things seem out of control
it's the best to love yourself.
Love, be your own philosophical perception,
be a reference by a question to the self
on the same subject.
Be your own focus.
The sense of self-hood
is never
your subjectivity.
Self-concept and
self-awareness
are only about
your true self and false self.

Real self is your tangible, dependable,
innovative and vulnerable person
and unreal self is your
idealistic, phony and pseudo self.

Trust your unprompted reliable experiences
have a feeling of being alive.
I am your real self.
I am not a rueful façade,
I don't lack extemporaneity
Neither I feel lifeless and hollow,
I am you, yet another 'you'.
In the game of Chess, the Queen protects
the King. In principle. Make me your
shield, you be my touch tone.
Love, loving me is as good as loving yourself.
I am your relationship with the 'self'.

I am your mirror image
Like a Siamese twin.
Make me your engagement with your self,
immerse in me and in me you engulf.

A Song Written Half and Half

The moon emanated early this dusk.
I wonder what he is discerning
the lonely moon.
In the unending celestial space
longing the company of his Muse
around whom he loops
day long and all night.
So far
too far. Yet so much to the core!
If not anything else
drinking the glowing night,
my pink lady, let me
get intoxicated.

Drink me to the brims and the lees
drink my musk and
my poignant meltdown.
You don't know what is there
on the other side of the fence
so have the luxury of the moon
go with the flow
rather than stand
in the mid of nowhere.
I never learnt how to win
what is not credited.
Nonetheless, I am capable of an
epic error in my character --
it's a cerebral exercise to
see the implausible,
a love, prized, cherished.

A Welcome World

*"Conflict is peace. Freedom is slavery.
Lack of knowledge is energy." – George Orwel*

Loving you is like going to the war.
I know I'll never come back the same,
I will either come home with broken limbs or
they send me dead.

I am fine with this welcome world my comrade,
because I didn't pursue love just to be in love.
I waited for the right man for ages rather than

waiting for true love from an erroneous one.
Neither you have any negotiable alternatives.
Loving me is your 'living', living as in 'breathing'.

I don't want to make 'peace' with life, if peace
is an alternative to this love, to this welcome world.
My ethics of war is a different floor.

The penalty of ethics-war is to help us to see
the alteration between right and wrong, and to underwrite
strategic dialogues on our public and distinct accomplishment.

Peace is not a lack of conflict but the aptitude
to beneficially resolve war as a momentous occasion
for evolution and greater empathetic action.

Peace has the potential to diagnose, honour, and unlearn.
Peace is a responsibility not to impair anyone, but it's the provender.
Big question is--is war imperative to bring peace?

Peace never means no contestations, no trouble.
It just means alliance. My war is not impartial commotion,
brutality, and an epidemic on 'their' idea of human rights.

War is obligatory before peace, only the degree diverges.
Let war break the crooked silence.
           When the status quo goes out of rheostat
and someone hits your human rights, war is required.

I agree love, the better you sweat in peace
the lesser you bleed in war. Trust me, to be systematized for war
is the modest scheme of conserving peace.

I am not a bird born in the cage. To me, hence,
flying isn't an ailment. Love, can this
war of freedom be a new beginning, a fresh start?

Ahalya's Waiting

"Ahalya, you will live here for many thousands of years,
eating wind, without any food, lying on ashes
and generating inner heat. Invisible to all creatures,
you will live in this hermitage. And when Ram,
who is unassailable, comes to this terrible forest,
then you will be purified. By receiving him as a guest
you will become free of greed and delusion,
you evil woman, and you will take on your own form
in my presence, full of joy."
Echoed husband Rishi Goutama's command
bestowed upon the beautiful wife Ahalya, who had just had
her first ever orgasm, the fulfillment of her
womanhood through Indra, in disguise of Goutama.
'Ahalya', the 'one with no ugliness'--
the woman beautiful turned into a stone there and then.
Reek of patriarchy with
the social game of victim-blaming began.

I am Ahalya. Am I really waiting since centuries
for my salvation by just a touch, and for my redemption?
I have the *Indriyas*, the five senses, inside me
so solid that I cannot be transformed to oblivion,
I am as inert as a stone.
While my acquisitive mind retorts, my steady mind waits.
I am the *Sthit-pragya Sadhak*, I have my *Indriyas*
in my own accumulation.
Doing my *sadhana*, I am time and timeworn.

Oh Ram, finally you are generously plentiful
to meet me, after ages of waiting. But my penance
is not yet completed. I will not consent
oh Ram, to be redeemed by you for an offense

that I have not committed.
I am untainted, confident and clean.
What purity on me will you assign?
What is the merit of this debate on of my pollution?

Oh the archetypal Ram,
if you really need to touch me, be the elemental man,
touch me as the elemental woman. Touch me
as the galaxies do collide, touch me with
all your unspent unbiased emotion.
Touch me as the blue firmament touches the stars.
Make me your lyre and lure me.
Give my harmony your personal touch.
I assure you, you'll solve the mysteries
of the universe with my touch,
because I am the quintessential, ultimate woman.

Your touch should be your creative language,
your behaviour, your basic attitude.
With my touch, stars ought to dance across your skin.
Your touch must take away my fears of
all Goutamas and Indras.
Love, soothe my anxiety and
fill my senses with your compassion.
Touch my cognizance and you can redeem the stone.
Make me your Muse.
You know, touch is where miracles arise
And exchange of the light and dark begin.
The curse of Rishi Goutama may be immobilized
with your touch, with this assertion.

My redemption lies not just in your touch
but in zero tolerance of
any marginalization.
I need a rejoinder from the society

and from you, oh the most knowledgeable one,
for my quintuple patriarchal relegation.
Father presented me, the puppet, to husband on his free will.
Husband couldn't fulfil me as a woman.
Indra tricked me to satiate his desire, not mine.
Inept, impotent husband cursed me
with what right, oh, with what right,
to become a stone exactly at a moment
when I was satiated as a woman!
And now why do I need yet another man, you, oh Ram,
to touch me and cleanse me of my uncommitted sin?

Touch sensitive, touch deprived,
touch-craving, I would rather wait till eternity.
I prefer to reject your offer of touching me
on the condition of taking me
into the snares of purity-pollution.
I am my own possessor, proprietor, I am my woman.
Let me remain ethically upright on my own terms—
this is my ultimate liberation.

***

Reference to Goutama's curse:
Splitting the Difference: Gender and Myth in Ancient Greece and India - Wendy Doniger, Mircea Eliade Distinguished Service Professor of the History of Religions Wendy Doniger, Wendy Doniger O'Flaherty - Google Books

'Alive' and 'Living'

"Can terms of endearment
few and from very far
offer solace, nay balm,
to our injured beings
when the world burns
countless pyres all around us?
And then I ask myself
am I not glad, grateful, to just be 'alive'?

Maybe those terms will accentuate the sadness
resonate emptily within
heightened consciousness of the distance
that cannot be bridged?

Even as these words flow out
I'm interrupted by mundane tasks
that must be done. And the world goes on.
The day will wear on until dusk.
And I'll think of you again."

"I hear you, love! I get your point.
The world needs to be healed with love and care.
But who wants to just remain 'alive', simply 'exist'?
Let *them* merely exist in your world
with their existential issues
while I live you, live in you, breathe you like oxygen.
our energetic collaboration keeps me going,
my friend philosopher and guide!
Please understand, the future is yet another country.
That's why I bring more to the table today than you are aware of.
I don't force myself to love or un-love you.
Life explores me and sends you
the messages through the universe

when I practice 'living' in love, hundred percent.
I have no defence mechanism.
My experience is more important than
perhaps what really is happening.
Since it's about me. I'll maximize this affiliation.
There's no gain no loss for me.
This means 'living' and not just 'being alive' to me.
By the way love, the way you get defensive about saving
each of our conversation on your computer, for imminent, is that
'being alive' or 'living'? If I may?"

Am All Ears to You, Love!

In this fairy tale of *La La Land-esque* romance
I am a minority within a minority within a minority
and still I maintain my tone and undertone even.

Alas! your love is so inconsistent that it borders on self-sabotage,
being potentially problematic since day one,
                    when you pulled the runner
from under my feet in the name of social custom.

You talk about things unswervingly more improbable,
so potent is its sourness that the aftertaste of each
                    hurt is equally odd.
Only the intimate love part of this unusual story feels earned.

Rest, is there any thematic tissue in it?
I know, love never comes with the guarantee of happiness.
But it's hard to accept truth when I think
                    all you wanted to hear was falsehood.

That you do not comprehend and validate truth,
                    doesn't invalidate it.
You accept some vague idea of veracity towards progeny
without undergoing it. It's like painting
                    a paper cake that you cannot eat!

Make that decision that may hurt your heart but heal your soul.
Deep down you know the truth, so don't carry the pain.
It will only leave an immense stain.

Learn to like the sound of your own feet
walking away from half-baked truth. I am all ears to you.
Do you know the variance between giving up and
                    letting go, my man?

I know if it is destined, love will find its way back to us.
The grim aspect of moving on is accepting the truth that you have already done.
Am all ears, but I refuse to entertain this pain.

Well, no pain no gain, no guts no glory, isn't it? I'll still find you at the
lost-and-found and be with you till death do us part.
An areological mistake, delusional, am not into the specifics of time, I follow the sun.

An Autumnal Duet

The night was stretched out
afresh watershed for me.
It squashed my eyes of slumber
then packed the hollows sniveling

and said, 'you have been acquitted
of all offences, and hereafter
you are at liberty
till eternity.'

Autumn, go somewhere you wish,
now I am numb.
The entrance to reveries
is padlocked for my faculties, just all.

You said, benevolent, 'ravaged by autumn
and hard blows of cold steel
I was shorn of my limbs
and my faculties numbed.

Upon strong beams
of a new sun
warmed by kindness
and incandescent smile

I have sprung back
in vivid hues
as your love filters
deep through my soul'.

And I Am in Love

I marvel every time
anyone tells me
that my reckoning
with my love
is one of volatile.

I pole to my own person.
Shadows shape and
reshape themselves
in me.
I know then,
I am in love.

Bottomless

To them, bottomless is *something that holds*
large amount of something.
And that there are plenty of deep holes
that exist, but none are truly, immeasurably bottomless.

Even the deepest pits have never infiltrated down below
the Earth's coating. To get something reflective
we'll have to use our thought process.

Ahh that suited my imagination of this kinship.
Love, aren't we in the state of affairs that requires
seemingly never-ending possessions?

For this bonding, bottomless are my roots and basis.
That is even a somewhat difficult and delicate process.
This rendezvous is the bottomless sea of our conscience.

I know, truth might be sunk in life's endless pit.
Yet, I am the pauper at your door with immeasurable winnings.
I have the appetite for our accomplishment that
                airs the bottomless.

Your eyes are bottomless brown pools, they drown me.
To live life, this is my bottomless colliery, my celestial source.
Though I know a gold mine is not a bottomless pit,
                the gilt disappears.

Bottomless shadows lurk in every corner of this craftily agreed
black-and-white nightmare, hinting at concealed revulsions.
Still, this day, this spring, you are my bottomless
                endowment of anecdotes.

Love, I never was solitary and possessed by
                            bottomless emotional needs.
This love is no self-indulgent bottomlessness.
My moods are immensely absolute,
              physical and metaphysical complications.

Your prevailing masculinity is my snare,
              and I don't want a release.
And you claim, my bosom is your
                    'consolation and stay', your only space,
my soul-searching love is your resolution and solution intense.

This bottomlessness is enormous in range, gigantic in nuance.
I am falling, falling and falling into this abyss.
My tormentor and redeemer, you are my tender hurt,
              yet you are the bliss!

Chamomile

The sky
an absorbent blue parasol
clogged with fragmentary pain.
And here I assemble myself,
half of my life consumed
by time
the other half soaked
in comprehension that
you'll never be there.

And yet I feel
your alarming presence
all over the place
in everything--
in myself
even in the clouds in the loves truck
azure.

In fact
you never did go away,
did you?
The love-soaked reminiscences
the cups of chamomile
engulf me
filling the void.
Yes, there, almost you whisper!

And then I come back, bounce back,
rolling inside myself
without
anyone discerning
far and near.

Day after Day

Day after day after day, coming to
'one hundred years of solitude'.

One month of loneliness, hibernation, isolation,
a month of breathing and just being 'alive', unconscious.

Is this indeed a fable of this pandemic?
Still I try to rule my mind lest it rules me.
I want to share quintessential poetry with you,poetry of
Amīr Khusrau Dehlavī, Rumi, Bulleh Shah,
poetry that is the fine flavour of life.
Enter my eyes,
I assure you, the moment you cross the threshold
of my eyes,
I'll shut my eyelids.

Alas,you reason that the admirers of a woman
'grovel' and plead for mercy,
you under reckon the heart's games.

Love,I agree, you are an elegant piece of
fragmented pottery,
put back, composed,by your own hands.
A perilous world juries your cracks
while missing the exquisiteness.
How you made yourself complete again
is the question of situations.
Same here love, our rapport
doesn't need to make sense
to anyone except us.
It's a strong bonding of just you and me,
and not a community arrangement
neither a project of public importance.

When you have something to speak,
silence is untruth, isn't it?
One of the most beautiful things is to have
your wounds heartened by someone
who doesn't see the flaws in your passion,
but transfers love into your body over the cracks.

I am that person who doesn't appropriate
into any rule-box,
I stay between the lines.
But my integrity is greater than any rule book
and stronger than even the blood vessels.
Living intact, in days and days of silence.

Love, sometimes those who try to bring you down,
don't realize that you are part of the purpose
that they are still standing.
What do you want?
If you say you only want
to live in peace and 'equilibrium' of your
house of bricks,, not home,
I should quietly get up and open the door of your house.
You will wriggle in agony, but writhing will be pointless.
Because by then there will be no alteration
between you and me, there will be nothing called 'us'.

Still, you are the earth I hold in my folded palms.
Any need that I'd be having, are paled
to the needs that you have.
Putting cold water on days after days makes no sense.
Love, some stories deserve a second chance.
And it's never late to do the right thing perchance.
Trust me, once you learn to speak,
you'll be forever free, so speak up!
I presume, everything is groovy at your end
in the midst of day after day after day of silence.

Debt

How effortlessly you said "I am in debt,
I am insolvent."

You owe a lot to me, love, you owe me a debt.
With this love, I want not just you
but the world
to think about me, yearning, *ahh what an enthusiast!*
I know, it's not an innocuous love.
It's devious, but for good.
I am life changing, but for good.
Certain things are better than good,right?
You just be an observer,
let me be the prime-mover.
Always watch everything
that goes on between us
and be insolvent, be more of it.

Love, you smell of wine
and faith and dependability.
You observe, I am kind of
a hunter-gatherer, always free spirited.

Clear your debt at the earliest.
I may move on without ever
being able to say a goodbye.
Another dynasty gone, another set of walls,
another terrace to look at the highways from,
more slender passages and vestibules.
Someday, you can only see me in memory,
till I fade there.
Is this how love evaporates?
Is this what you call your 'debt'?

The numb enchantment of time is a carnage
since
the outbreak of the pandemic. It has cut us off
from our salad days, and it is so mundane.
It's confiscating our branches, our roots,
and the people who made us what we are
the individuals who completed
our reminiscence and history.
And the impending days look beyond access.
Is this what you call 'debt'?

Jaan, you are right, we're lucky to just live
heaving into a fragile extant.
To breathe as long as our lungs permit,
as long as there is oxygen enough for us to fight fit.
All other magnitudes of the stint have evaporated.
Now I only embrace you in your dreams,
Is this want you call 'debt'?

You ask me to stay hidden
and be only in nostalgia.
You claim,
"I'll always get back to you."
Love, storms also get tired,
the pandemic will get exhausted soon.
Do you really want to wait till the end?
Then, what if I free you of this debt?

Dreams, these days

Dreams, these days, are of the moon and moon-manufacturer!
The gripe translucent skies in the night
the mood swings of solitude, the cognizance of the air, purer,
the memories of missing moon motif, a vanished delight.

Dreams, these days, are of the sea and the seafarer.
The uncluttered, sweeping ocean epitomizes much more
than an unbiassed body of water; it embodies a malicious elegance
that never hesitates to induce the narrator.

Dreams, these days, are of some make-believe love
                          and some eternal lover.
Ahh! Genuine love is measured by how deep you tumble
and adjudicated; mediated by how trivial you are,
                          how willing to scuttle
just to save it and make it linger.

Dreams, these days, are of a comrade and about some paramour.
It is resolute by how keen you are to unclutter.
Offer your conviction. It is generous, incredible
and apparently very kind. It is, of course, often biased,
                          it is colour blind.

Dreams, these days, are of travel and the traveler.
The wanderer and the wanderlust,
                        the reminiscence and rumination.
Do not foldaway lost travel stories to the hermit's harbour
there is a great lot you aught to see post contagion.

Dreams, these days are of many lands,
                      many homes and the homemaker.
There is boundless share your passion daily does sought to travel.

You needn't unpack right away, keep your luggage at bay.
You are not parting, your authority shall you take back, oh seafarer!

Dreams these days are of a long life-- glorious, happier,
                            healthier, better.
Still, if you succumb, the show goes on even minus you,
                            so don't despair.
Dream anyway, love anyway; you shall soon find
                            your 'home' awfully closer!
The marvels of the mourned sound colossal;
                            they may, as well,entice and lure.

Epilogue

"To love is to burn, to be on fire." – Jane Austen

After the homily today, the much-needed discourse,
after the tête-à-tête after eons
I had those heart-in-the-mouth immersions.
I apostrophized you, my paramour,
and contemplatively recollected the vivid feelings
that we had before ages.
The heart brimmed, eyes teemed, soul abounded.

When you said
thinking of me is 'an accidental impulse',
I of course didn't take that fabrication.
You know love,if you live to be a thousand-years-old,
I want to breathe a thousand-minus-one-day
so that I never have to live run-down of your love.
I love you as certain clandestine things are to be loved,
surreptitious, between the sleuth and the soul.
Despite your I-don't-love-you edifice, I know, I always know,
that you have been in love
increasingly, and then all at once, the way you fall numb.

There was a time when I thought that you were perfect,
and so I loved you. Then I knew that you were imperfect
like me, and I loved you even more.
I love you for what I am when I am with you
not for what you have made of yourself,
but for what you have assembled of me.
I love you for the fragment of me
              that you fetch from time's womb.

Love, thinking of you keeps me wakeful.

Fancying you keeps me benumbed.
Being with you keeps me thriving.
You are essential to me like the heart needs a beat.
I love you and it is the commencement of the whole lot.

You make me wish to be a better person.
Love, now we know, love never dies a natural death.
It dies because we don't know how to restock its foundation.
It dies of blindness and blunders and perfidies.
It dies of ailment and lesions; it dies of inertia, of acerbic ruination.

But then, now I agree with Theodore Roethke,
"Love is not love until love's vulnerable."
Shall I call it the epilogue of love, or a new foundation?

Everything Looks Small from a Certain Height

When life slays you a bit every day
you seem to be slipping away from my fingers
all the time.
I wish I could fix the picture
and not let it slip away
to the height I cannot trace.
I know,
the winner takes it all, the loser stands small.

And I have heard them say,
likes of you decide, likes of me abide.
Even then,
even when I look at all things small
from a certain height
let me face my Waterloo
myself without wherewithal.

Tonight, a vivid carpet of red Gulmohur
took over the earth
as if tracing
a juvenile paramour.

Eyes Well Up

"I love walking in rain because no one can see my tears."
-Charlie Chaplin

Eyes well up in joy, exhaustion, happiness,
orgasm, edginess, expectations, sulks.
But my favorites are those
that come from our never-ending
incessant laughters.
Till our muscles ache.
And those from the overpowering
emotions that I feel
just by watching you.

Love, don't brood over today's tears
wake up tomorrow stronger than today,
let's face your fears.
After all, welled up eyes are
a sign of implicit contentment.
And maybe, a smile is
the sign of some silent, ancient ache!
Tears are, in a way, prayers.
Tears are bottled up passions.

You know love, no one merits your tears,
and the one who deserves them
won't make you cry helpless.
I have learnt it the hard way--
tears are not adverse sentiments.
After all, my tears gave me the metier
to turn hurt into forgiveness
and forgiveness into love.

It's time we didn't cry in rain anymore.
Let the eyes be washed in tears
so we can see life with clearer views.
Tears are a language, they dialectally evolve.
Love, let's go hand-in-hand and celebrate
the places we have cried in the past.
Let's change the narrative.

Eyes

Silence is the language of God.
All else is poor translation.
--Rumi

'Every word has consequences. Every silence too!'
-- Jean Paul Sartre.

I cannot really do any much about it.

They say they are intimidated by my wide, dark speaking eyes.
Questioning, interrogating, argumentative eyes?!
Well, eyes do not really have to be docile, compliant.

Eyes are truth.
Eyes do all the talking when I deliberate
my words are
not as powerful as my thought.
On such junctures, I just let the eyes silently articulate.
Words need not always bother to frame a judgement.

Of late I discovered a thing or two about eyes. They melt.
They melt even without tears, and they get teary
out of nothing in the midst.

There are a few things that words cannot say in enchantment.
Sometimes things get jumbled since words cannot
designate what not and what to accept.

But then, one cannot speak within the self
and let the words bleed in silence, just quiet.
The loudest exclamations are heard
 in silence if we listen prudent.

Silence is peace. In absolute silence, I hear
the poetry of earth. Silence, unveiled with eyes,
reveal the undertones of the heart.

You cannot really do any much about it.
About eyes, I mean! Eyes are caught
in the dichotomy of a subdued certainty and concert.

Filling the Molecules

Loving him is inhaling a thousand roses in spring
knowing tomorrow the air will be unfeelingly untaken.

It's like enjoying a poem
or like swaying with the harmony of a song.
While filling the molecules with blossoms.
And marvelling at the symmetrical flocking
of birds of a feather
and the glory of a ladybird
caught on his camera at dawn.

Like an inconceivable sense of sorrow
wishing to weep quietly
are the countable-uncountable moments
of such a love.

Alternating between enticing and exasperating
alternating between euphony
and cacophony
the words turn into a
hollow boom.
Of such a love.

I just want
During the moments restless and restive
to fathom his secrets
and know
if there's a ludicrous yearning,
a cyclone raged in his heart too,
A grief-soaked love
echoing mine
of such a love.

Or, it's just an agenda
of love?

Or is it, alternatively, a
mind immersed in meditation,
likewise?
Carrying a volcano in the heart
of a mind roaming in some desert?

For me, love doesn't mean alms or empathy.
It's moderately an absolute surrender.
'Take it all.'
Like an offering in a shrine.
On the altar.
'The whole thing please!
Leaves, buds, flowers and all.'

There hasn't been another
loner in the world
who looks for life, filling the molecules.
Who wants to fly and dissolve
in the lonely void of darkness
of such a love.

A module of easy-torment, this love.
A stubborn assessment, such a love!
Pain and contentment underscored, ah love!
Underscored with double thick lines, here and there, this love.
Aware of all upheavals of the world, such a love.
Touching the mysteries of life, ah love!
Believing that pain purifies all, this love.
Thinking, pain too is a gain, such a love.
Such incredible a love.

In fact it's so incredible a vision! Unambiguously
no parallel between a life of love
and other lives.
Neither one can emulate it either
and nonchalantly move.

Fluency in Silence

You dictate me the poetic lines in absentia
I am just the amanuensis to write your poems.
You call me 'word-wizard', but you are the art of wizardry.

The moon may teach you, it's fine to go through phases.
And the sun says, no matter how many times
you go downcast, keep rising in the sundry.

One has to consider the kind of silence one follows.
If you don't understand my silence, how do you claim
to understand my words who are free birds that fly?

Silence is to the spirit what sleep is to the body.
Silence is healing. Right tongue comes out of silence
and right silence comes out of speech, you know why?

Silence is an ocean, speech is a river.
Meaningful silence is juxtaposed with hollow words.
Silence is the language to encounter divine.

Love, my silence is better than proving a point at this point.
The quieter I become, the better you can hear.
My fluency in silence can sort out our subsists.

In any case, you must win, I prefer to lose.
If you win, you are the conqueror; if you lose,
you still are the captor.
In any case, my love, you win, silence wins.

From Ocean to Ocean

And you started with a proposition,
"I thought life was complete, life came to a full circle.
And then there was this oceanic blue rain.
Perchance I had forgotten love.
Perchance life was droning.
But see, now new streams are flowing into me
from ocean to ocean,
from salt to sweet water."
And then I whispered,
"My quests end in you, my desires flow into you.
You are my politically incorrect allusion.
Shall we create
our hall of memories
with some resolution here?"

Ahh, my merman!
Majestically liberated,
the bay amplifies out into the sea
to pacify its lordly peninsula, spasm its seashore,
calms its surfs to a silent shimmer,
then succumbs itself to a complete whole
to ocean›s inexpressible delusion.
Form ocean to ocean.

What does my goblet of ocean cleave to?
You may ask me!
I am the story of
grandeur of purple and spangle of gold.
Warm greens and blissful blue
inoculated with the sunlight through
unruly ripples that idly roam
here and there.

Plummeting waves with gallant foam
sands and pebbles that chase and go ashore.
Shaman currents softly slide
potent magic charm of the epochs old
this does the goblet of the marine hold.
A universal hoary gray
with rigging of sand array
to keep it from obliterate display
in the track terrestrial ashore.

Love, have you seen our concourse in the sea?
The streets with no abodes to vault them,
and only the shadows around them!
Yet running as straight as can be
sallow in the blue,
corresponding too,
stretching afar
larger than the bar
in the atoll and far away
further than the arch of the sheltering bay.
Love, have you seen the avenues of the sea?
Grey pitch, and greyer ocean
surf alongside the coast and in my heart--
They itch your name
from ocean to ocean.
My lips need not speak anymore.

When sliding down the Atlantic, the colossal,
I witness
storm-wind like the Phoenix.
Landward in his fury he scourges
the ocean surges
weighed down with weed from the crux.
Night hails and stars their wonted music carry on
in malleable bottomless nadir of the firmament

in a mystical blanket of in distinct obscurity laze.
The vast stretch of the subterranean
the hoary paths of moonlit snooze
the mount and drop for ever pensive
with the splendid heaving of the maritime.
Night will approach very soon
with tenfold darkness where the sinister is so abrupt
black waters will become back waters sooner or later
in a land-locked yowl.
The sea cliffs slide down the blizzard rambles
yielding the abysmal nap
in the glossy the frothy margin, white as snow,
reverberation of smother echoing rising away
midnight carping of captive waves.
There is some yearning in the untrod den coppices.
There is an ecstasy on the solitary shore.
There is this civilization where none encroaches.
By the deep ocean, there is music in its roar.
I love the Pacific no less
but the Nature that produced 'him' more.
Recite our conferences, where I bargain the core.
From all I that may be someday, or I have been before
to mingle with the Universe with this texture
what I can never decipher,
yet I cannot ever, ever recover.

You heard it all and said, "My blue lady, you have arrived
to live and love, now and here. And
forever.
Your oceanic blue is my inundation. I am
flowing from ocean to ocean!"
I smiled back. I think loved back too.
"You are just me, yet another!"

Haiku Poems of Love

Star
They are keen to know why am I a star
so bright. This is how it glows, a scar,
when it snaps into the scheme of light.

Rhyme
I rhyme like poetry
to spot myself in the large frame of time
and to set the dusk resonating, in our projectile.

Poem
You said, *love, anything for you, my truth eternal.*
Take me, take heart — take it all. I glinted--
Make love to me like a poem, if at all!

God
He conferred upon us a new directive:
love each other, just as I love the Universe.
Now everyone will know that you are my cohort.

Faith
The mountains may alter, the peaks may be astounded
but my faith won't move from you,
and our agreement of peace won't be dazed.

Life
Through your unwavering love
I am granted interminable life.
I will be so, as long as you are the 'last leaf'.

Prayer
Prayer is the sacrament of gratitude.
My only prayer is gratefulness to Him for the existence of 'us'.
My solitary prayer is 'thank you', and nothing else.

Half of Her Lovers are Half the World Away

Men who loved their wives and those who did not
all fell in love with her
when she was simply out and about in the world.

Her 'men' knew, she was the brimming vessel with
      an eternal capacity to pour.
Well, she didn't think much about love,
neither of the 'safe' love-loves, nor of any loves in the conflict zone.

Her dry sardonic wit made them only fall in love
      more with rationality.
Lost in time, with the audacity of hope,
      she was found in eternity;
turning her wounds into wisdom, an expert at the law
      of diminishing marginal utility!

She wanted to be forgotten from their collective memory
when she had to wait to watch the slippers of couples
      in front of the Taj
while the couples were clicking away 'couple-pics' to glory.

A street urchin poked a hole in her story
      in the midst of a deadly inner silence.
"Won't I even be allowed to wander lonely like a cloud? Ahhh!"
She, of course, had her many longings and belongings.

Her 'men' every so often left her drained, high and dry.
Some other times they cared to say a proper goodbye.
In any case, she didn't judge them, she just did low lie.

Her self-introspection and serious reflection
                    were a caricature of living-loving.
Her faith was bigger than fears with time's
                    intoxicants in her hands.
There was no wind in there—just air to protect her
                    'men' from fading.

Above her outer skin, there were wordless walls
with a fistful of sky. With time, invariably,
her men turned into distant memories.

She wrote the stories of many a life,but
her own story lay buried at someplace in a vault.
One day she lost the keys to that treasury that
                    she had carefully concealed.

She had that habit—
save the best for the last.
But much cared-for-stuff from her wardrobe were always lost.

Has Tomorrow Enough Time?

"Today will die tomorrow."
— *Algernon Charles Swinburne*

Isn't it nice to think that *tomorrow* is a new sun
with no slip-ups in it yet?

The undying in you is conscious of life›s timelessness.
I wonder why you don›t go to bed justfor a snooze contented.

With the new day comes new metiers and new thoughts
close your eyes and let me embrace you unsurpassed.

Tomorrow you will pine for this day.The finest homework for
tomorrow is doing today your best, your newest.

Days gone by are not for you to mend,
                              but tomorrow is there to win or lose
only certainty is, you don›t know what is going to materialize.

Yesterday is ancient, tomorrow is imminent, but today is the aptitude.
Love, wake up each morning, and choose to be happy
                              or choose to be blue.

Unless some appalling catastrophe has occurred the night before
it is pretty much up to you.

Tomorrow morning when the sun shines through your space
elect yourself to make it a happy diurnal.

A decent design for today is better than
                        a picture-perfect plan for tomorrow
don't pause for an inspired ending to come abysmal.

Work your way till the lees and see what comes up
love, you are the sum total of your knowledge systems.

Life's experiences, be they beneficial or undesirable
make you the person you are, at any given point in you to subsist.

Like a flowing river, gather those experiences as moss
for those yet to come with me will rewrite the person you stand.

Even I am not the same as I was before we met
nor will I be tomorrow; I cherish the 'me'
                    you rewrote with amendment.

This is my call for tomorrow, I don't lose my poise,
because from today, only today, tomorrow will originate.

Rainy days still make us wet with tears
it was pouring that rainy day, you were all smiles,
                    the day we met.

My panacea, my liberator, I learned the art of 'tomorrow'
                            from you
you forgot that conveniently, after having me taught!?

Historical Baggage

A conglomeration of mysterious, formidable,
vaincohabitates take the centre-stage.
A carnival of fast-talking, quick-thinking,
hollow-headed, rule-revolting, vodka-swilling people
who plague mankind on mid-air! Ahh how baffling!!
Reduce them to a tag. In order to triumph,
you must first adapt and then ask them
to become better.

A pressure-cooker troposphere where
people are pot holed against one another.
It's a room where *Karva Chauth* is still an entity
of farce and melodrama galore.
A bigot's historical baggage, right?
Where are the modes of
'live and let live' I wonder.
It's remorseful love,
I guess it's a tough question for you on gender
and human rights for sure.

Hymn to Chant

"And to 'scape stormy days, I choose an everlasting night."
— *John Donne*

Anticipate love, pray for love,
command love, dream of love,
put your life on hold in the making of love.
I did it, all of it.
I thank you for reacting to my litanies
at the right stint.
Now I start and culminate my day
with your name;
you sent me this hymn to chant.

Love, it's time for the warrior to be fought for
and for the devotee to be loved
and of course for the vessel to be held.
To flower stalk my windy days,
thanks to you,
I pick this undying night.
This hymn is my amazing grace
in the bleak midwinter night.

Yes, this tranquillity is sore, but if I endure it
I sure will hear the rhythm
of the perfect cosmos.
You don't need to say it,
but the room is spread out
with that kind of blessing that I chant.
It's the amalgamation of loss and profusion.
I still chant the plenty that has no guilt
the loss that has no hit.

You extemporize passionately in my chant.
This music is your handmaiden.
Come what may, I will still love you
with my unabridged, awful, contemptible heart.
Because I love you to the segregation of all prayers.
Now let me live plentiful to die at love's feet.
The cup is full and brimming,
now in bidding adieu there's no regret.

Love, this hymn has emptied me
of all that I was so full of.
It emptied me of I, me, myself
and filled me with you, all of you.
I live in your elegance, sans ego,
and confirm your love to all I meet.
This redemptive chanting is
my character pummelling isometrics
my ego-battering exercise.
A glowing woman now I am,
let me help you to glow.
In this chanting, I remain aglow.
You are my hymn and your name is my chant.
I am, unquestionably, resilient.

Introspection

Manna of life for me
no-boons for you
up keeping for me
sans any care for you.
Why not work on the same page?

Maturity for me
naivety for you
considerate for me
no such sentiments for you.
Love, golden moments don't knock twice!

Surrendering for me
self-doubts, yielding for you
life cycle as a method for me
decease of finesse for you.
Ahh, why not deliberate from the same box?

Life is calm for me
composite for you
time sings back to me
and the universe holds things back for you.
Just a thought --why not share my melody?

Is Something Left?

As I got down from your car
you looked askance, *is something left
on the car seat?* After all you
have to be observant, and go salubrious
to your other world
to your other 'other' self.

A world that you think is of full
of my virtual presence, a world where
I follow you invisible, invincible, everywhere.
A world where you are not 'valued'
the way you merit, the way you say I make you feel.
A space where you have self-doubts about
your being so special, so unique a man,
and so very unresolved.
I understand, I make it clear that you are special,
you are a man of power, sympathy, humanity,
compassion and you are so full of passion.
Love, what if there are no patrons for those virtues
in your other world, I am waiting here,
for all your love, like a lover and a pauper.

As I was pondering over those thoughts,
I tried to recollect if something is left in the car?
Nothing left Love, I am vigilant not ever to intrude.
After all between us there is no such 'arrangement'.
We both are confident and transparent.

But what about my fragrance in the car that you so adore,
and the hints and tints of those stolen kisses
when traffic lights were blurred?
What about the hours and hours of long drive

holding hands at the car gear?
And what about the unspoken, implicit visions of growing old together?
What about a lifetime of pledge and obligation?

Island

Darling, this is your poem,
and let 'your' world read it just as a
poem-poem;
no indulgence no clemency required.

With a deep sigh, you say,
you're my island
my escape from cacophony
where tranquility pervades
a stillness
punctuated by your beatific smile
and your caresses.
Oh what is this malady
that refuses to leave
this vile scourge
remnant embers from hell
leave me listless and filled
with an unfamiliar lassitude!
When will I be back to myself
when will I go back to mellowing elf,
to my life, love, happiness--
to your arms, my better-half?

I wink frivolously, coquettishly and ask,
"by the way, darling, who all are
battered by our love?
What trader's massive vessels
have your moans sunk?
Who states that your romantic tears
have flooded their island?"
Then I dizzily chose to pick your
lips, eyes, nape, neck, earlobes,

your handsome atlas and axis, one by one,
and nibble, peck at each, engrossed.

But then you go on and on—
ahh my love, you don't know
the foul ways of this world listless.
They shatter our dreams with malice.
You know honey
I can die for it, if not live by love.
Take me the way you like
make me your slave.
But tell me tell me
how to handle the world
how to keep them away
from our golden island
where just me-and-you
you-and-me
live-love uninterrupted?

But now, I get indulgent,
permissive, passionate.
Gliding from your neck to your bosom
to your body masculine that never ceases to tempt,
alluring, tempting, ardent, islandic-fervent.

I just whisper, like Donne, with a glint,
'For God's sake, hold your tongue, and let me love!'

Isn't Love Enough?

Isn't love enough love? Isn't love enough
that you quest for everything else that should matter so little?
You know, the world anyway makes and breaks one and all.

Afterwards, only the survivor becomes solid at broken places.
Because love is the most agreeable way of discounting
                                    a broken piece.
And because, only birds born in a cage think flying is an illness.

Love, see a world in a modicum of sand and
                                    heaven in a desolate flower.
Let time decide who you meet in life.
Hold eternity in the palm of your hand and perpetuity in an hour.

Your own emotion decides who you want in your era
and your own pronouncement decides who stays.
Rest assured, your secrets are safe with me,
                             I can't remember my own passwords.

If you don't correct the world when they dismay you, and ill-treat,
they will never learn how to treat you right.
In any case, you have to fight fit, you have to defeat.

The truth is that you will lament forever,
                             if for you love isn't enough.
Sometimes you will not get over the loss of the loved ones,
but yes, you will learn to live with it, on and off.

You will heal and remake yourself around the loss
you have agonized. You may be complete again,
                             but you will never be the same.
Nor should you be the equivalent to the one who you left amiss.

Love, love did never hurt you. Someone who doesn't diagnose
                                    the ways to love,
hurt you. Don't confuse the two.
With true love, either you forget everything or
                                    you evoke who from the who.

I shall anyway re-read you as my favourite book
                                    at different stages of my life.
The plot will never change, but my perspective of love may.
For me love will be enough, nothing more nothing less,
                                    just any given day!

Looking Elsewhere this Spring

"In the depths of winter, I finally learned that within me lay an invincible summer." -Albert Camus

The right person will love you
even after you are eloquent of all your flaws.
The wrong one will blame you
even if you bounce with your best.
Your culpability is their gain.

Anyway, once the tempest is over, you won't recollect
how you made it through,
how you accomplished to endure.
You won't be certain per se
whether the storm is really gone.

Because one thing is there.
When you come out of the tornado, you
won't be the same one
who got into the storm.
That is what this gale is in and on.

We make the life we need, isn't it?
Give yourself the permission
to immediately walk away from immoral vibes.
There is no need to explain
or make sense of it. Trust your impression.

Meet yourself from my point of view,
you will see this.
What you are seeking is actually seeking you.
Because you see less about yourself
and more about me within your inner voice.

I assure you, from here
we wouldn't leave empty handed
even after the slate is clean. If ever, that is.
Let's look elsewhere this spring. After all
within us lay the invulnerable choice.

Metaphors

Of late I understood that
the language, designs and metaphors
I had been using for life
were not judiciously worth.
I thought, I need not give in too much
to feelings and emotions.
And that, a visibly sensitive heart
is an unhappy possession
on this shaky earth.

You washed away from my soul
the dust of everything commonplace.
You knew, I am the virtuous marshal,
and I lay down my life for the ewes.
And you made me realize
my religion, arts and sciences--
they are twigs of your tree.
My words are but morsels
that tumble down from the banquet
of my awareness.
You wanted my memorandum
to be perceived by the world,
you said, it has got to be directed.
To keep a up lighters weltering,
we have to place oil in it.
Did I tell you, I have tossed
my cap over the wall of that space?
As you wished, and as you wish!

My conscience is my constant Christmas.
I am grateful to you love, you are
the amiable gardener who makes my soul blossom.
Your very presence is a prodigious poem.
Now living is a happy dusk and a new-fang led street.
I fill the pages of my poetry book
with the breathings of your heart.

My conscience is my compass.
And I am grateful to you for all this knowing.

Museum

On the wrinkles of my face, may the story of your life be encoded.
May my word wizardry be your speech pattern.

Like in a museum, let time be transformed into space
Life never intended to make us perfect man and woman.

Because whatever is perfect, belongs to a museum.
Don't get so abstract, a fog is no doubt rolling in, but don't shut down.

The present is a museum full of artifacts and art.
Just that, we forget to open our eyes, and keep them blissfully shut.

Your no-game game must be the most popular of all,
I understand this silence as an interlude of clarity.

May I call this phase an intermission
love? Is the glass half full now or the glass half empty?

You have got this quality of slightly decadent surveillance.
It's paralyzing, musimizing and like your cold-blooded heart.

You have, anyway, seen me at my most vulnerable souvenir.
If I could objectify our love, it would be a keepsake in a gallery of art.

That's my short version, you majestically claimed.
And the long version? Why don't you cut the long story short?

You are so striking, like some Pietà by Michelangelo.
For optimal loverness, you are too handsome and fledgling.

But your eyes look lost, and not so much worldly.
Anyway, a little other-worldly will do, that would be your piety.

You're so hard on yourself, you live like running in a museum.
You entirely redefine standards of self-sacrifice and self-pity

Love, a museum is a place of ideas and integrity.
In the museum, walk slowly but keep walking diligent.

Let us rather build our own museum of contentment,
not just of bricks or art pieces, let its thickness be humane and compassionate.

I am that museum, revealing to you my lifetime love.
I am your work of an era and domicile; I am your immortality.

Don't measure the success of this museum just as an work of art.
Hold me between the landscapes, like a pedant live in it.

My Moods, Modes and Mores

Then I giggled and said
"baby I can be witty,
flamboyant and coquettish.
You have to master the art
of handling my myriad moods!"

You chuckled. Winked.
"Oh I see!"

Then you held my hands gently and took me
to your magical island of wishes.
Smeared my body with tender
yet passionate incessant kisses.
I had no other choice
but to go for a submission,
all over again, to your quests
while I soared in you
and guided you to my
unseen depths.
You just inhaled-exhaled-moaned
and discovered the unabridged me.
You sighed in utter amazement
sheer incredulity,
you marveled at my abundance.

Love,I cannot tell who from the who--
the prime mover and the admirer,
the victor and the vanquished.
In this inclined love
we merged as the ocean and the rivers.
There was a torrential twinge in the abdomen.
Body quivered, numbness in concentration.

I entreated, "isn't love
enough, love? Why torment me in such profusion?"

You traded virtuous-innocence
and enthused me, the wild stream.
Then guided me to the isle
where I no longer distinguished
my culmination and your initiation.

This time you giggled
at the bewildered, unnerved me.
You graphed penetratingly
my moods, modes and mores.

My Tranquil City, Tonight

Is it fine with you, love, to live and negotiate
through the language of oblivion?

It's a separate matter that
this is yet another love story for you.
And you can tell us, re-tell, re-tell more tales.

Some know parts of it, some not even a hint of it,
some compose their own editions of it.
Anyway,I remember the primary version of the tale--
that clouds froze in dark nights.
Despite your claim
that I took your story and turned it into
whatever I needed to.
Fair enough,to make the world contented
of late
you began to amend
a simpler, happier life for yourself.
Fair enough, love!

I am glorious.
Proud.
More proud.
Much more, tonight.
To love you is like going to
the battlefield.
One comes broken, bruised
from the battle, for sure.
Still I feel like a lepidopterist, who has
Gloriously peeved an unusual moth.
We couldn't have been written out of the past, right?
I know that you know that I know.

The untold and the told, I know it all.
Predictable, comforting, heartening sorrows,
but trustworthy, consistent ones.

Tonight
my city is tranquil;
as if the city is having its meditation classes
as if we all are gleaming from our Yoga sessions.
Tonight
the sky is the woodland of stars.

I wonder,
is another world possible?
Ever? Ever?

Life failed me in a nebulous yet fundamental way.
Let me embrace what you have given me
like we embrace old friends;
let me deal with your gifts like
we handle old enemies.

Perhaps it's raining in my head
perhaps it's my survival strategy.
I know that you know that I know.
This is how it has always been
between you and me.

I made you so tall, I needed to,
in order to live life;
and thus, you always act
as if I owe you a thing or two.

We have been simultaneously
sweethearts and former sweethearts
siblings and former siblings

lovers and former lovers
friends and former friends.
When it comes to the matter of heart
we always have had
an implicit jungle of safety nets.

Your knowledge has made you pessimistic;
your intelligence, tough and callous.
You think too much and believe too little.
And love even less.

You are my salvation, you are my nemesis.
In you, I have been swimming through layers of love.
With you, the heart suffers like a grey pebble
in an accumulating stream
rolling down, always in motion.
I have been your beloved madcap.
You know why. I don't need to tell.

I knew love, the macabre, would visit upon me.
So you did.
We knew that we knew that we knew.

And then the Judgment Day had been forestalled
a blessing received its place.

I wish life could be minus such determinations
and death minus such finality.

No Next Birth

Every time you recede
with an unassuming proclamation
'we will meet in the next birth',
I dissent.
You leave a vacuum in my core.
But every time you attempt
to retrocede
you perpetually come back.
Yet the vacuum shaped
by your narrative of
next birth
is never filled up.
The vacuum is a relic,
the helical lies dormant.
The space
of no-next-birth
dangles in the air
suspends in the judgements
and
it lingers in tumult.

Promise of Profusion

"And then her thoughts were the wind."
--Origins

I love you for myself.
And I love myself for you.
Love, love yourself half as much as I do,
you'll see the spring. Just try it!
Get in touch with life again.
pay attention.
Don't settle down. Who knows,
what is there for us
in accumulation?
Take my crafted thoughts
floating stories
hundreds of memories, woven poems.
My life has
sedately witnessed it all.

That, somehow, got you teary eyed.
All those days and months and years
you were hypothetical
in swinging eternally
between delusion and illusion like
the pendulum in the old clock.
This new-found contentment
this new life with me
became your redemption.

Take it all. And ask for more.
Take my promise of profusion.
Plethora of feelings
excess of love
abundance of life

take it all, and ask for more.
Tread slowly, don't
customize yourself
I have already tailored life for us
in profusion, manumission, liberation
and reclamation.

Reaching the Island

Today
You talked about this hurt.
Yes, hurt, and its peeved wave.

"My rambling
impetuous utterances
hopelessly misshapen
inadvertent and impulsive.

When they reach you
the random scratches
transform
into soothing words capes
filled with serenity
and bursting with hope, decisive.

I'm the clay to you
my potter
I willingly capitulate
to your ministration
nay, I surrender
my very being to
you my love."

I got it, I understood.
Love, go, reach our island, there I await.
Don't bend, don't water
the hurt so well. Don't oversee your
own soul conferring to
their manner. Rather follow
your concentrated passions
hardheartedly, and move.

Only once you are alive.
And young, only once.
Only once comes such a love.
You know, I don't measure, don't weigh, I just
give myself to you, simply give.

There's nothing more intense
than whatsoever for me you have.
I know, where there is intense love
there is also penetrating disquiet
concerted hurt
lurking beneath the exterior designs
of urbane encounters, divisive.

Reverie

"Hazaaron khwahish enaisi ke har khwahish pe dam nikle.
Bohatniklay mere armaan, lekin phirbhi kam nikle"

Clandestine concealed hollering
decoding the decorations of your cognisance
and of course my conscience-- ahh a
capricious canopy overlapping!
Seasonal-sauna, swinging-singing
cut into quizzical moans, winded wings.
Mingled-mixed-magnanimity, previously veering
tarmacked sandstones
crawling out of their plummeting moralities
those plunging dipping cliffs.
Their smothered tongues and wrists rebounding
quercouscons unconcerned burlesques
of deteriorated appendages
wobbling revolutions.
Now our souls twisting turning
souls actually slavering
through their ceded cacophonies and discords
cleaned and cleansed complaints
pompous soul-screams
mugged at the stratums
the reveries.
Ghalib's quests to comprehend
the actuality of the considerateness
and civility of the
shaking nibbling bobbling edifice!

Shipwrecked Souls

Yes, true that.
Life is a shipwreck—but are we anticipating
to live in the lifeboat?
All my life, I did wait.
Waited for someone kind, not only in the
commencement of a camaraderie when
life seems bright
but also when things get hard.
Waited for someone to respect my boundaries
give me love without keeping count.
Waited for the one who inspires
me to be a better person each daylight.
Someone consistent
with his efforts in showing me how much he cared.
Someone who wants to be a part of my world
making me a part of his.
Someone who lets me know that I am in his mind.
Who makes me feel easy and calm
like coming home.
Who doesn't cloud me
because his actions may not match his arguments.
Who strives to protect my heart
choosing me over and over again.
Someone imperfect, but real, rare and special.
Because perfection is an illusion, real is the thing.

You understood,
two ship-wrecked souls encountered
hereafter persistently and harmoniously to sing.

Small Things Big Things

Unfair silence, unapologetic quietness
small things, very 'small things'
that I have been ignoring so long
in my dormant conscience
were nagging me
to have a dialogue with myself.
I apprehend, silences can be more prevailing
than
actual dialogues
breaking free from the social mould
to the half-baked, rushed
personal impersonal relationships.
These things have been
age-old, without hard questions.

Unsettled I had been with the
if and buts, left with
an ode to my womanhood.
Sometimes lenience to
the so called big things
are most patronizing, isn't it?
They are like
unheeded melodies.
You told me, loud and clear,
the real thing, the 'big thing', that
the queries shouldn't be where is my home,
where am I from, but
where do I feel at home.
I understood,
empathy lessons were
the need of the hour.

Some But's are So Telling!

Love is the main motif, as you say,
but then, the public station precedes matters of your vein.

If you need to win this battle, you need me as your army,
but, you claim, it's your lone war with some disdain.

Perpetrator of injustice, my nemesis, foe, adversary--
isn't this 'but' a reverse psychology, for one?

Some buts are so emotionally invested
they rush so much on the fifth gear in the brain!

How much ever you take precautions,
but they are sure to crash, day in.

But's are but intangible concepts--
you just cannot see the impending tangibles, you are time-slain.

My twinkling dreams are essentially both earth and sky,
but then the rain clouds are askance derision.

Hearts are the biggest battlegrounds,
do not hold on to the but's, they're time's condensation.

Love, rivers do not go reverse; better mend your
fragmented, disjointed, telling but's, and move on.

Spring is the Season

Introspecting my long silence
I rehabilitated my passion into compassion
and got into the Spring season.

Now, Spring is ours, it is the only season
of rich abundance and completion,
because you healed me of the torments of epochs unknown.

Healing process wasn't calm, it was hard-hitting, tough
but you knew, you always knew, that
Spring was in the offing, Helix was anon.

You are right,there's a chasm between what we want
and what we can have. But love, don't go down
that lane again, each piece of dark cloud has a bright line.

They said,*don't wait for someone to bring you spring.*
Plant your own orchard and embellish your own soul.
Spring will eventually be your season.

But I did wait, until the first shades of Spring came to me
with your whispers, 'you are my only poem'.
Then, blossom by blossom, my Spring began.

I am indebted to you love for this beautiful aide-memoire
that *I deserve a Spring as I am obliged to nobody for nothing;*
am grateful to you for unlocking the floras to paint our smiling loam.

Now witness this, my love, my comrade of the Spring--
I am your earth, I gleefully familiarize to the embraces of the sun
and witness the fallouts of our amatory canon.

Love is agreed upon the wind. Watch out for soaring passion and deepest desire whizzing by ourcranium.
Ahh, God created Spring and the same day he created optimism.

Love, let's have faith inthe process and in the seasons of hope.
Yes, winter had been tough, but now Spring is here.
Let's get restored every single day in this budding season.

Stitching a Love

I am stitching a love, clothing a camaraderie
building a door through which you can enter

walking with the wind, facing
history and taking in my stride the time's talon.

Our days are nourished with the needle and the thread.
Our sewing home-base is our happy abode.

Our darned love tells our cherished tale.
Striking possessions come composed, one stitch at a spell.

What I style with my needles, I bounce with my heart.
Any day is a great day consumed by our needlepoint.

Stitching a love – it's not just a dexterity, it's a healing.
Love, we have to collaborate in this webbing.

I am merely a strand of it, minus you I am nothing.
Whatever you do to my web, you essentially do a therapeutic thing.

Love, stitching is symbolic of hale and hearty human features,
stitching a love, you are darning our pasts
                      and edifying future prospects.

The Fleet-Footed Polar Deer

I said,
I love you because the entire universe, to it,
did conspire.
You just smiled.
I chattered then, man's only true contentment is
to live in anticipation of something to be won by him
for his near and dear.
You smiled a little more.
I had more to say.
Worship something to be deified, and love something
to be prized, forever.
"I see!"
Then I prattled,
I used to hold a singular view, in which
I wished for only 'experienced happiness'
of those substances, and that indulgence is
an imperfect approximation of
factual contentment
without any anxiety and fear.
You were silent, looking deep
into my eyes. Though I couldn't hear
something that you did whisper.
Now I had to chuckle at my own expertise
and wisdom unlimited.
Then I said,
my love, love is the alliance
caught on fire.
Now agree? Or is this too bizarre?
"Yes I agree, my
fleet-footed polar deer!"

The Lotus Leaf

I am the lotus leaf. I am ardent.
Nothing can hold me. And
I want to hold on to nothing. I have ultra-hydrophobicity
as unveiled by the leaves of 'Nelumbo', the lotus!

Drop something on my peripheral, it floats and cascades.
I have been making the mountains float since decades.
I am the backwaters of Kerala, I recede
as much as I ensue and proceed.

My lotus-effect denotes to self-cleaning.
Dust particles picked up by water droplets
by the micro-and-nanoscopic architecture on my shallow
diminishes the droplet's adhesion to my surface.

I am conceited being seamlessly unsoiled.
My heart is impeccable, so are my passions and my soul.
I hold on to no anger, no greed, no jealousy, no callousness
and no love, no desire for that matter.

"Love, you are self-cleanser, self-made, self-motivated.
This is your forte; this is your character.
You can be hydrophobic or hydrophilic, be whatever,
depending on how the water gets on to your exterior.

I comprehend and I adore you for that staple.
I won't pour anything into you as you are not the vessel
to drop my indistinctness thence .But can I be your lotus stem
to support you, hold you straight, upright and fair."

The Maps to Reach You

"When feelings are immense, words stand poor."
From the blue you said that, you, my cherished blue-eyed lover.

You traveled all the way from the island realm remote
I knew, you knew, that is the time when
          the drinking glass had to be fragmented.

The glass of the mellow and all-encompassing wine is to calm.
What goblet is in my hands?
          Which map takes one to you, my chum?

Suddenly the Yellow Moon is full. Tonight
you hang like a silver smile on my lips, you pierce me abysmal.

This city sleeps on the pavement. They say a charmer will
          cross the asphalt soon.
Planting his chauffer, he will disappear to the air thick and thin.

Hauling on my city's dusky fabric the chauffer is vexed by sea,
          sand and salt.
I see, you raise your hand to touch the Yellow Moon in amazement.

Just to intoxicate you a bit in a little-eyed
          window of the *lover's nest*
just so you'd be evoked by taciturn glasses and
          the street I connived.

Standing in the lattice of silence, I am water lily,
          I cling to the portico
I think of you like ease and breeze, my acerbic
          downcast face as you pass through.

In the hall of my longings you belong,
              I smile and make head lamps wink,
in these demanding days your envoys take
              to the place you'd never want to go.

Because you never knew to want more,
              and because I introduce you to you, tacit.
Wait and watch, our blue sky will gradually grow
              thinner and solvent.

Let's put their lights out, aware and unaware let them sleep.
All I know today is, in your presence I am good to go,
              let them peep.

Good to go and climb to the summit and reach
the Terza Rima of my wistful wishes and pivotal,
              infinitive desires, deep.

The Sea of Pedigrees

True that.
A bottomless embrace is the response
even when the
question is mysterious.
It transfers sustenance, security, keenness
guides and glides harmony apposite
from body to body, soul to soul.
Merging animated
sans questions
charms the senses and touches
your passion.
This, only this,
is panacea of the cosmos, the creation.

You whispered these honeyed words in my ears
when I bit your earlobes
in a deep embrace.
I floated in the sea of frenzied dreams
and dream visions
when you futilely attempted to explore
the nook and cranny--just all of it--
of my body beautiful.

It's not easy my love
to touch the mysteries of the ocean.
And I smiled prevailing.
You seemed to be at some solution.
I looked deep in your eyes.
I could essentially see your
desires of pedigrees
unfulfilled, unattended, unrequited.
Instantly I took charge of
your dreams, wishes and your subterranean passion.

I whispered, 'take me as you like me,
it's a complete surrender.'
You assumed I was right,
and you preferred the act of capitulation.

As I merged with you in you
and mocked to be asking for clemency
you smiled honored.
You said, 'you aren't seen nothing yet lady'!
That was my triumph! Making you the man,
the elemental man, was my resolution.

Now the memory of that moment is my safekeeping.
Ah, I have to rather safeguard it
lest time's talon corrupts it
in my myriad day long mundane action.

The Woman that was Me is Gone

With this, the woman that was me is gone.
Love, me-or-not-me should be something
that you want or you don't, take your call.

I'll never be happy with just a part of you,
still, offering me a part of you,
you can deliberate.
I just want you to do what you want to.
You before me, yes love, it's always been so.
I am a woman in transit, with a stopover
in your life.
Trust-broken, yet again
I am trusting the world.
Well, because I guess, love is not a lonely pursuit.

I ask time, are all wounds actually healed?
For sure?
I have the tension of being inside,
while knowing that I am never an insider.
And this fear of being recognized.
But then, my fears give me the incentive.
My fear perpetuate my biases.
Flying and falling become my attitude.

Love, I had been constantly at war with my body,
making and breaking it.
There was no stopping over.
I thought I knew everything I wanted.
I was never that damsel-in-distress
who was convertible.
This is a grey area though, you said so.
Tell me, is regret better, or gratitude?

You conquer, exasperate, cloud me.
Because I let the woman that was me, evaporate.
I fuse with you, my Muse.
I agree, only life is priceless today, this day.
And each day we live, counts.
And love is patience.
Living on your little response or
non-response, knowing that
love for love would be the answer at the end.

The woman that was me is gone. Long gone.
I live with this trepidation--
do faces fade with absence?
What if I wake up tomorrow morning
and don't remember your smile?
Will you, then, be a forgotten folktale for me?
Will the woman I let go of,
still hold on to you, and just be?

Will she ever be her phoenix?
From her foundation, the woman who I uprooted!

Time, the Quiet Witness

Times of absence, blue and dreary
clad in grief's shadowy array.
Times of quietude, witness of weary
subtle feelings of the soul, eyes teary.

There is an apprehension in the firmament,
an aspiration of the breeze, and a movement,
the five elements are a period and a hint--
it's sure some cause for a lover's unsound judgment.

When our ancestors are homegrown, we have to reason
their righteous philosophies, else it would be incredible
to bear them. But when they are absent, we soothe
time for their absence by lodging on the memory of a
superstition.

Love, then why are you so quiet? Your silence is
a feeble fibre that the deceitful air
of the contagion wanes. Your speech was once so impartial.
The quiet time is the witness to our love's labour, erroneous.

If what time says is true, contentment is the absence of malaise,
then I will never grasp pure joy. For I am haunted
by a fever for consociate and experience,
I am the witness to time, the quiet witness.

To Laugh Like You

"I possibly cannot meet you next week."
You said that with some reflection.
"Why love? I thought you love meeting me!"
"Ahh yes, but it gets difficult, you know the way of the world!"

I mocked oblivious and yawned to your never-ending fears.
But then, you came back to your inventive paramour moods.
When you are around, nothing matters but
                              the intimacy and the titters.
You giggle to anything I say, you make love with aplomb.

My world is so unlike yours, I realize.
I have nothing counter to it, I fine-tune with
                              your amusing anecdotes.
I see some tags ring a bell, and you are pointlessly alarmed.
Then I tell you my two-ears theory, that makes you chuckle.

"You know why I have two ears?"
"Ahh yes, perchance to hear, to listen ,my sweetheart?"
"Not *eggzactly* that. To hear with one
                              and to throw out from the other.
Selective hearing is the best, filtered
                              judgements work a miracle."

You again giggle and say, "I so admire you for this power.
You are like the sun, you only take the best out of the worst."
And then you beseech me to guide you on our meeting next.
"Meeting you is so inevitable *Jaan*, so very imperative!"

I scratch my Sherlock Holmes head when you are busy kissing.
                          I open my think-tank
and my expert brain, with my signature style -- *all-is-well*.

"Yeyyyy!! Coming week you have an important
                              General Body Meeting!"
"Oh yes Ma'am, let's get serious about today's mating…
errgeneral-body-meeting!"

Sure I have a funny bone love, I sure have.
But you activate that with your elegance, so naïve.
You tickle my funny bone with your interminable giggles.
You make me 'me', you 'woman' me with
                              your infectious manliness.

What I love the most in you love, you know,
                              is that, you don't just laugh
to 'save tears' as Charles Lamb would ponder.
                    You laugh like a child.
You laugh like you, you make love like a pixie, the world seems
a better place when we are laughing glorious
                              even in the deepest embrace.

Touching You

"Touch comes before sight before speech.
It is the first language and the last, it always tells the truth."
--Margaret Atwood

You touch my body, you divinize it
your touch calms my mind and restores my spirit.

You know, there are three thousand touch receptors
                       on your finger tips?
Love, with your touch you touch my whole personae,
                       my mind and essence.

No other form of communication is as wholesome.
Your gentle touch is petite and easy,
                       with its echoes it does come.

Until you spread your wings, how will you know,
                       how far you can soar?
Love, do not judge me by my scars of the past or my faiths,
                       or the gods I adore.

Know the content of my heart by my touch,
                       that's your tactile education.
Minus your touch, life is a slipup,
                       your touch is my emotional lifeline.

Let me take your rainy days, touch you deeply,
                       and make the raindrops
glisten like diamond. You know, touch is far more
                       crucial than my other senses!

It's myriad times stronger than verbal or emotional contact.
Your silent sensual touch does profoundly
              awaken me to God's perpetual court.

I have a heart that never toughens, a temper that never tires,
and a touch that works like soul penetrating reimbursements.

Of all the gifts you can give me, the gift of your
              touch is the most precious.
Through your hands you convey me a kind of radiance.

A warmth oozes out from your inner fire, a wrap for my nippy,
a light for my dark, with apiece touch,
              you make me immensely happy.

The first sense to ignite me is your touch,
              it is the only thing to tingle my depth.
Love, long after my eyes betray me,
              your touch will remain faithful to my earth.

In the recitation of life's final exoduses,
              we often talk of losing touch on our strive.
Like Michelangelo let me say, "To touch can be to give life."

Truth and Gospel Truth

Ancestors walk through time, holding hands
making me see truth.
I see the clans went away, no near and dear left existing.
Nothing is eternal, by design the world is a dream.
Live it thrust, copiously, for
it is now or never.
In the name of gospel truth
you leave me a sky full of clouds.
The truth is, calm seas
do not necessarily make a perfect sailor.

You invaded my heart and left it paralyzed.
I understood
the unadorned facts without elaboration,
as in the unvarnished truth
grossly misunderstood for gospel.
You believed it absolutely, viewed as truth,
as in you took every word of them as gospel,
but in fact you are often blemished,
your doors are left ajar.

Love, someone had to say it!
You take some fabrications for gospel.
You are privileged that you can lie low.
You take truth down a peg, take it for a ride, and then to
the mat, to the woodshed, under your wing,
up on the entity called love. You take truth wrong
you place it by storm, though something is amiss,
you take it as it comes, on face value,
then you take truth by the throat,
and you take it down a thousand, down to the studs,
take it for a spin, take it in your stride,

take it in tow, take it lying down,
take it off the table, take it on board,
take it on the chin, take it on the nose,
take it on trust, take out in trade.
You appropriate truth, you make it
a truth of convenience, of accessibility,
a gospel truth of your manufacture!

We have Earned Our Tomorrow

There are two versions to it, isn't it love?
One—the road ends here. And the other—
we have earned our tomorrow, ahh yes, we have!

You must own your actions in this rapport.
That initial thrust in our bond
in the direction it was launched can be our forever support.

Love, I have been trying to get into your interstellar.
I see, all you need is enough fuel for survival.
And now, I confess, I am beyond redemption.

I am sure, you will carry me from apartment to apartment,
from relationship to relationship, even to your tomb
just in case you succumb to destiny's bizarre design.

Mooning over tea, kissing me deep-deeper-deepest--
these are the moments that will wash over you.
If you chose the road taken by all, this sure will happen!

Just knowing that I exist somewhere may suffice for you
you are that prodigious, inordinate a lover.
But for my living, the presence of the *physical-digital 'you'*
                will be certain.

Unfinished, untested, unlived love won't work for me.
Love, don't carry the social-responsibility-torch so bright
that it burns you, burns 'us' from our life's canon.

Don't you don't you dare send me there and
spin me into an alternate persona, I am on an impromptu mode.
Let's rally to keep the game alive till time and timeworn.

Because this game is not about winning or losing.
It's about playing the games that the heart must play.
Jaan, hold your life, play up and play the game!

It's not that we have nothing in common, let them
engineer that, you need not succumb.
A small portion of time cannot reflect life in its entirety and sum.

Don't deal in extremes. Let's be the idyllic illustration
                         of negative capability.
Because we are at the same level of energy and ideology.
                         I am in control
of our lives. Let's underplay, understate, because today
                         we earned our tomorrow.

When I Wiped Your Tears

'If you feel pain, you're alive.
If you feel other people's pain
you're a human being'.
  -Leo Tolstoy

Who says, 'men don't cry?'
I told you about my earnest feelings, teary eyed,
you understood, yes you did, and implored me
not to cry. You got restive.
It was all about me, my hurts over things inadvertent.
My tears were oozing and exuding.
Just then I had a swift look at you.
Without any much fuss, without ever talking
about your hurts too, your tears were rolling
dispassionately, silently from your hazel eyes.
That stopped my sobbing, my 'protests', and I
wiped your tears.

Love, you never looked for the person who
you thought will make you glorious or feel special.
You believed, you were the one
who was going to make a happy world for us.

It's so natural to feel one's own pain,
but your ability to texture the other person's agony
elevates you to the man so special.
Your gift of sheltering my tears over my pains
in your eyes was my healing course.
You made a succinct point to capture, amend my rulings.
Empathy is the key word— in your unwritten space.
Your unspoken words held, there is a big difference between
human-being and being-human(e).

Somewhere I read, if you let
other people's problems be your entire focus,
you are co-dependent. Love, is it fact?
However, all you silently did was
you transformed pain into ecstasy, with your Midas touch.

No man is an island.
Now who says, 'men don't cry'?
The calendar of wisdom doesn't.

World Within A Tree

Planting a tree,
we grow with it in gratitude.
Like they say, *'you are
as kind as a tree'*, in veneration to no end.

To cut the long story short,love, this space is enough
to fold my wings.
Your bosom is the tree to shelter me.
My last resort.
You are privileged to be the forbidden fruit
from the forbidden tree.
But I ask,
why should anything be forbidden, anyway?
You are comprehensive like a tree,
incorrigibly romantic and quixotic.
Like a tree, you forgive foes and move forward,
yet you always seem benumbed
with the mayhem around.
If you say *I am sorry*, I say *I am not God*.
Don't say that to me. I am only a magnanimous tree.
This is our micro world within the tree,
that is what we will leave behind.

Sometimes I get immersed
in my own establishment.
I unexpectedly run into you,
it's a bit of a surprise, it takes me a while to adjust.
Like the squirrel and the Robin-Red-Breast game on
the tree, that is.

A civilised society is one in which people plant trees
under whose shade they will never sit.

The *Great Law of the Haudenosaunee*,
the founding document of the Iroquois Confederacy,
the oldest living partaking democracy on Earth
says-- "In our every deliberation, we must consider
the impact of our decisions
on the next seven generations."

Precisely, I do it.
Love, I have planted our tree,
just grow with it.

You are Another Me

"Tread slowly love. Let's take no burden. One step at a time."
That's when I knew, you are becoming another me.
You love me with a love that is far beyond love.
You remind and recap --we fit like hands and the glove.

You are another me when you love the moon
and starlit nights, and when you believe in the universe.
You didn't 'fall' in love with me, we walked into it
gloriously, hand-in-hand, that was the unsurpassed move.

You are yet another me when you believe,
                    we aren't destined to do things
planned for us by the universe. You rather have the conviction
that we can make things work, make things happen
the way we wish, we are the makers of this sieve.

My privilege is-- you are me and I am you as cascades blend
with the brook and the brooks with the sea. Then
the gales of ecstasy assort forever with a honied passion.
Nobody is solitary;all mechanisms fall in place
                    in the law of divine love.

My Muse, when you grow old, take my poetry book by the brook
and think of these moments when you wounded me with your
nonchalant stories of worldly snags and questions unsolved.
I encounter resolutions but you don't pay attention to receive.

You will remember, how many loved your treasures, their 'rights',
and how many loved the pilgrim emotions in you. You will
for sure find a long queue in the memory lane on one side
and solitary me on the other. Then for me you would crave.

Till then, you are another me, and I live-love-breathe you.
I wish I could be your changing facet of life; I wish I were.
But no qualms dearest, time is the greatest master,
time takes over all that is somber and gray,
                          time is all that we deserve.

You Before Me

"I am my own muse, the subject I know best."
--Frida Kahlo

When you feel dead inside, and if you are a lover
you gotta counterfeit happiness.
When you have self-doubts, and if you are a lover
you gotta put 'you before me', always.

Love, love yourself first and then the universe falls into line.
Self-love seems so often unreciprocated
though to fall in love with yourself
is the inventive underground to happiness.

Self-love is not self-seeking, egotistical; you cannot
truly love another until you identify the way to love yourself.
Owning your own chronicle and loving yourself
is the bravest thing that you'll ever safeguard in due course.

Love, can you transfer me love from an empty vessel?
If you're incisive for that one person
who will change your life, look at you,
take a look in the mirror of my eyes.

Thus, you are legalized to be both a masterpiece
and a work in progress, concurrently.
You before me, you are unrestricted, you are prevailing,
you are love, you have the worth, you have a purpose.

In the *Bhagavad Gita*, it's deliberated, you were born to be real,
and not to be perfect. Realise that you are not made for anyone else.
You are complete when you are autonomous. You are your own.
Let me get stimulated by how you are in agreement with
imperfections.

The real human struggle is to avoid being overwhelmed
with how you think about yourself.
No one is you and that is your influence, your supremacy,
that is your relationship with fair play and justice.

You before me—this sets the tone for every other
affiliation you have. Falling in love with yourself
makes you indestructible, imperishable, therapeutic, miraculous.
That is the narrative of our extreme insurgency.

You can Never Unknow Me

"Man is not what he thinks he is, he is what he hides."
— André Malraux

Just because something isn't falsehood
it does not mean that it isn't illusory.
But one who voices sheer slices of truth
in order to swindler is a craftsman to obliterate.

Conflict is based on trickery.
When we are able to manifest, we must seem inept.
When using our forces, we must appear indolent.
When far away, we must style trust that is adjacent.

Seldom, very seldom, does comprehensive reality belong
to any human revelation;seldom can it materialize
that something is not a little disguised or a little incorrect.
Oh, what a tangled web we interlace when first we exercise the art!

Never try to do whatsoever that is separate from
who you are. A forced smile is a mark of what
feels off beam in your heart, so recognize it when it transpires.
Living a fiction will not let you unknow me for sure?

You Own a Piece of Me

Love, you own a piece of me. In our entwined, tangled fingers
when you clasp my hands into yours
in the car, in a careless care.

You own a piece of me when I offer you my bright black mole
and make-believe to take yours. I say, "I am yours
but never mine you are!"

You look at me askance, why not?
"Ahh you belong to the universe!" You smile and whisper,
                  "but this is the
divine agenda of the universe, this love is my core."

Of the many reasons that you won a piece of me, here is one--
you can tell me there is a little bird
trapped in the dishevelled branches; all the people

flouting it because they do not know
what to do with it except for leaving it alone
till it frights itself to a decease premature.

You set it free, you take the bird to open-air
and write to tell me how language feels hopelessly inoperable
if equated to the bird's scare.

You own a piece of me then, love. But you are mistaken
language is all we have, oral and otherwise. Your silent
language of care for the little creature is your behaviour.

You own a piece of me when we live-love Nature,
when for the planet earth we dearly care.
And then you make me the earth and suck my musk,

you own me, I become the woman of mud.
                In my incessant bleeding into the
menstrual cups and in the softness of my rather firm breasts,
my lineage, ancestry, obligation, my womanhood I offer.

You smile askance, tell-tale at me not to be so formal, so proper,
and thank you so often. You own a piece of me then, all over again.
Then you claim,I am your 'word wizard',
                and the art of gratitude I master.

Your Familiar City

"I am a bud, pulled off the branch.
Where is my reclamation?
I am Mira.
Oh Krishna! You are elsewhere
in the thoroughfares in your chariot.
My feet stirring to a conduit unversed
but the tap-tap of each heartbeat
every string of my being
is constrained in the sludge
of the artery's rib cage.
Amend me like a limestone's sculpture.
Place me in your familiar city.
The night has stretched out
afresh watershed for me.
It squashed my eyes of slumber
and packed the hollows with blubbering
You have been acquitted
of all offences, and hereafter
you are at liberty, till eternity.
Go somewhere you wish, rouse and benumb.
The entrance to reveries is padlocked."

"Expanses have not yet twinkled, Oh Mira.
The delusion dynasty is quiet and benign.
From the bonfires of fiascos
and disillusionments
let the legends
of the approaching new beginnings
remain indefinable."

Your Fragrance

Of all the things I've lost to the contagion,
I deliberate upon your fragrance the most.
In the absence of your comforting embrace
and enticing fragrance, there is a piercing loneliness.

I am unaided with my griefs, memories, regrets
and just your fragrance. There is no shoulder
for the bereaved me to cry on.
You are too distant to bounce back with balm and solace.

Love, you are my entire world, your fragrance preserves my curlicue.
My days are measured by the moments of waiting,
my mission every day is to count the days, because the absent are
never without liability, nor the present without defense.

Bravery is to battle with fear, control of fear, not absence of fear.
Time off sharpens love, and presence strengthens it.
Your fragrance and the mole on your neck are my antioxidants
and my fuel,
if desolation is the absence of your fragrance, then let me distinguish.

I am possessed by a malaise for knowledge, most empathetic,
that is into the making of your enthralling shape and the incense.
Real charm of this businesses of the hearts means an absence
of judgment of others, says in absentia your intoxicating fragrance.

Distance from those that we love is self from the self,
it's a deadly deportation. As a gullible animal, let me trust something--
in the absenteeism of any good grounds for credence,
must I be contented with the reminiscence of your fragrance?

Black Eagle Books

www.blackeaglebooks.org
info@blackeaglebooks.org

Black Eagle Books, an independent publisher, was founded as a nonprofit organization in April, 2019. It is our mission to connect and engage the Indian diaspora and the world at large with the best of works of world literature published on a collaborative platform, with special emphasis on foregrounding Contemporary Classics and New Writing.

www.ingramcontent.com/pod-product-compliance
Lightning Source LLC
Chambersburg PA
CBHW020540080526
44583CB00013B/921